I WENT
TO THE MARKET

I WENT TO THE MARKET

an old Czechoslovakian folksong
retold and illustrated with woodcuts

BY JOSEPH DOMJAN

a Bill Martin Instant Reader

Holt, Rinehart and Winston, Inc.
New York, Toronto, London, Sydney

I went
to the market
with a brand new penny.
I bought
a pig,
and I still have my penny.

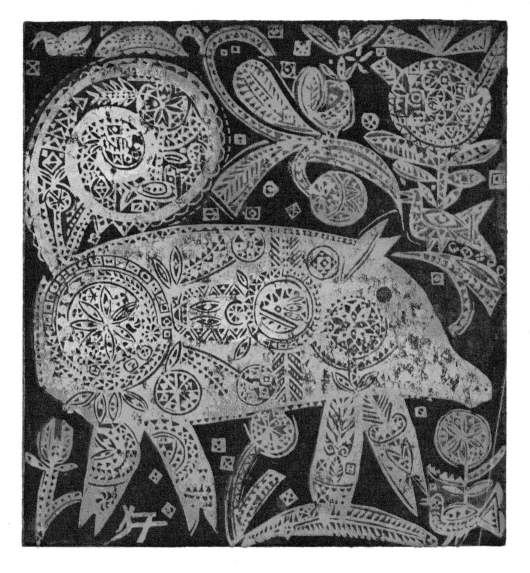

I went
to the market
with a brand new penny.
I bought
a peacock,
and I still have my penny.

I went
    to the market
    with a brand new penny.
I bought
    a rooster,
    and I still have my penny.

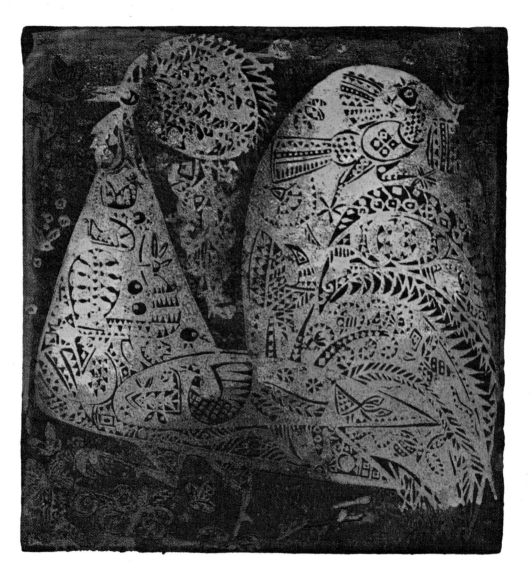

I went
        to the market
    with a brand new penny.
I bought
        a pony,
    and I still have my penny.

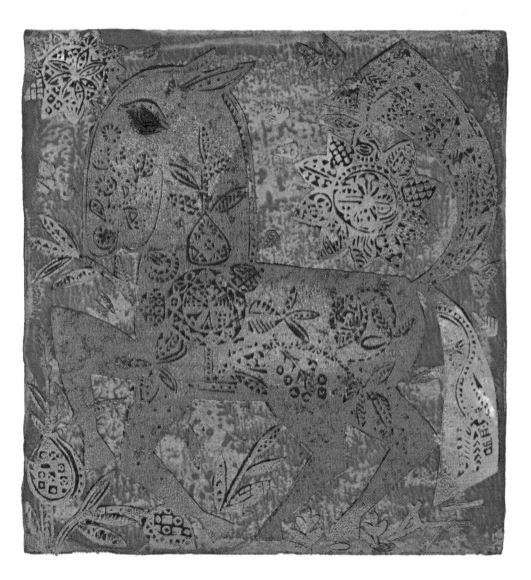

I went
   to the market
   with a brand new penny.
I bought
   a deer,
   and I still have my penny.

I went
　　　to the market
　　with a brand new penny.
I bought
　　　a dove,
　　and I still have my penny.

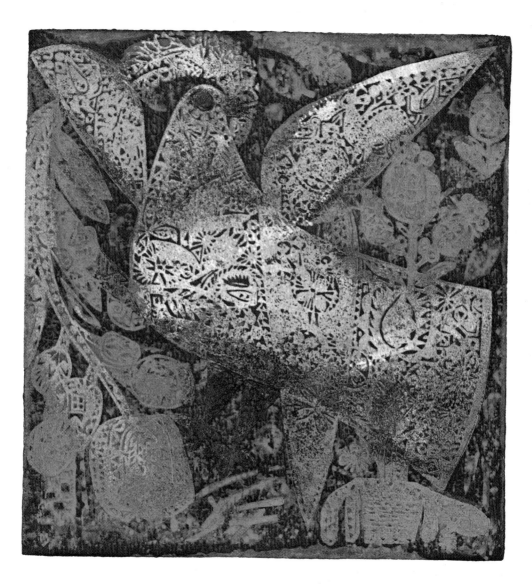

I went
          to the market
     with a brand new penny.
I bought
          a turkey,
     and I still have my penny.

I went
    to the market
    with a brand new penny.
I bought
    a dog,
    and I still have my penny.

I went
        to the market
        with a brand new penny.
I bought
        a queen bee,
        and I still have my penny.

I went
        to the market
    with a brand new penny.
I bought
        a lizard,
    and I still have my penny.

I went
     to the market
    with a brand new penny.
I bought
     some flowers,
    and I still have my penny.

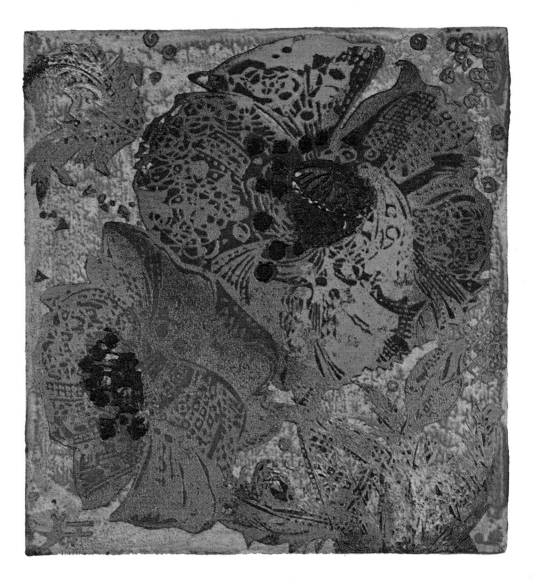

I went
      to the market
   with a brand new penny.
I bought
      a dragon,
   and I still have my penny.

I went
    to the market
    with a brand new penny.
I bought
    a boy —
    now I don't have a penny.

I have a pig,
    a peacock,
    a rooster,
    a pony,
    a deer,
    a dove,
    a turkey,
    a dog,
    a queen bee,
    a lizard,
        some flowers,
    a dragon
and a boy—

Who needs a penny?